Independence
Day

Independence Day

Graduating into a New World of Freedom,
Temptation, and Opportunity

MICHAEL DiMARCO

Revell
a division of Baker Publishing Group
Grand Rapids, Michigan

Hungry
Planet

© 2012 by Hungry Planet

Published by Revell
a division of Baker Publishing Group
P.O. Box 6287, Grand Rapids, MI 49516-6287
www.revellbooks.com

Printed in the United States of America

Library of Congress Cataloging-in-Publication Data
DiMarco, Michael.
    Independence Day : graduating into a new world of freedom, temptation, and opportunity / Michael DiMarco.
        p. cm.
    ISBN 978-0-8007-2069-8 (cloth)
    1. Christian youth—Religious life. 2. High school graduates—Religious life. I. Title.
BV4531.3.D565 2012
248.8′3—dc23   2011038067

Published in association with Yates & Yates, www.yates2.com

In keeping with biblical principles of creation stewardship, Baker Publishing Group advocates the responsible use of our natural resources. As a member of the Green Press Initiative, our company uses recycled paper when possible. The text paper of this book is composed in part of post-consumer waste.

12 13 14 15 16 17 18   7 6 5 4 3 2 1

Contents

Powdered Wigs
and Falling
from the Nest

It was the summer of 1776. Our country had just declared independence, and I had just graduated from high school. Okay, I didn't graduate *that* long ago, but sometimes it feels like it. For me, graduating from high school was my Independence Day. All I ever thought about was becoming independent and moving out of my parents' house. Don't get me wrong, my parents loved me, but I just wanted freedom and all the opportunities that came with it. My parents had random rules like no watching TV after they went to bed, no leaving the clothes dryer on if everyone was leaving the house, and no making fun of my sister. Oh, the bondage! After I graduated, even though I was going to go to college in my hometown, I couldn't wait to move out. So two high school buddies and I got a two-bedroom apartment, with Crazy Eric converting the dining room into his bedroom.

No curfews.

No parents.

No siblings.

No food in the fridge.

No hygiene.

It was awesome.

After twelve years of being forced to do something (school), I was now independent to do what I wanted when I wanted. At least if I could afford to. Moving out of my parents' house was my declaration of independence. And I declared my independence again when I bought my first car, graduated college, and got my first good paying job—all little Independence Days. But my high school graduation was the first big one. Of course, my idea of independence was way different from my sister's. Her idea of independence had to do with money and security. So she didn't move out until she was in her mid-twenties, and that was only because she had gotten engaged and didn't want to move directly from my parents' house to her married house. She wanted to "check off" that she had lived on her own, even if it was for only a year. So while she lived at home for free, she worked her tail off, bought the things she wanted, stashed cash, and put up with the crazy house rules as a trade-off to achieve her financial independence.

So what comes to mind when you think of independence? Guys with powdered wigs signing a scroll with ink on the ends of eagle feathers? A slave freed from the bondage of a cruel and immoral master? Or maybe just something simple like getting the keys to your first car?

Before defining something, it can be easier to recognize what it *isn't*. Like how figuring out who to date usually starts with a list of people you definitely *don't* want to end up with. So here's a list of words that are the opposite of independent: dependent, subservient, constrained, restricted, enslaved, helpless, subordinate, weak, infirm, invalid, incapable, debilitated, disabled.

And here's one more from *DiMarco's Thesaurus*: unawesome.

That's what dependence feels like—sometimes even if it's dependence on those who love us and raised us. When we're children we're dependent on them to put a roof over our heads, feed us, clothe us, drive us, insure us, sign permission slips for us, and be legally responsible for us. But before I accidentally make an argument for people not to have kids, let's jump to a definition of what independence *is*.

To be independent is to be free from outside control, self-governing, capable of thinking for yourself, and self-sufficient. In less dictionary-ish terms, it means choosing where to live, what to eat, who to be, what to become, how to achieve all that, and why it all matters. For the achievement-oriented person reading this, it sounds like the perfect life. For me, the where to live and what to eat sounds freeing, and

11

the rest sounds like a lot of work! But that's what comes with true independence.

In fact, one of the biggest myths about getting independence is that everybody wants it. Truth is, just about everybody *says* they want independence, but when it comes right down to it, not everybody wants the work that goes with it. Think about it: Who has more worries, the girl who has to do everything for herself or the guy who just does whatever he's told to do? Let's face it: We want the car but we don't want to pay for the insurance. We want our own place but we would rather get free rent. This is why momma birds will eventually nudge their babies out of the nest; the momma knows that a bird that never leaves never soars on its own, and so it never really becomes a bird but just stays a worm-eating nest ornament.

So whether you're scrambling to get out of the nest as fast as you can or you feel the cold, sharp beak of a parental in your back pecking you to your edge, independence is coming your way, whether you're ready or not. And this book is here to help you deal with the three major things that come with your first taste of independence:

- Freedom
- Temptation
- Opportunity

All three have their upsides and downsides. Yes, we *are* going to talk about the upside to temptation! But first things first. I want to give you a pop quiz. Before you scream "Noooooo!" just calm down; this is an easy one. Here goes:

Good Riddance (Question #1): What's the thing you're going to miss the least in your life after graduating?

Oh Wait! (Question #2): What's the thing you're going to miss the most?

Can't Wait! (Question #3): What are you looking forward to the most after graduation?

Don't Go There (Question #4): What do you fear the most about life after graduation?

That's it. Easy, right? What you're probably going to find is that those questions and your answers to them have a lot to do with how ready you are for independence and how you will handle freedom, temptation, and opportunity. But to show you that I'm with you and not against you in this quest, let me tell you how I would have answered those questions as the seventeen-year-old me (yeah, I was a young'un when I graduated).

What was the thing I was going to miss the least in my life after graduating? I already mentioned it, but living at home! Seriously, just too many random rules that didn't make sense.

What was the thing I would miss the most? A lot of my friends, some of my teachers, and I guess how comfortable I was at my high school. I wasn't super popular, but I was popular enough that school was fun.

What was I looking forward to the most after graduation? For me it was "finding the one." I really wanted to have a family young since my dad was already retired with gray hair at my graduation ceremony. I didn't date much in high school, so I was ready to get my date on and get married.

And the biggie: *What did I most fear about life after graduation?* Not knowing what the heck I was doing! That and constantly changing my mind about what I was going to be when I grew up.

Okay, I share my answers with you not just to show you I'm a good sport but to tell you that in a lot of ways, my biggest fears *were* realized and my biggest hopes *were* dashed. And the reason was that I wasn't ready for the freedom, temptation, and opportunities when they came. That's why, powdered wigs and birds falling from the nest imagery aside, this book is not only a gift from a loved one but also a gift from me to you. This book is the one I wish had been gifted to me after high school graduation or even college. The lessons are the same and the stakes get even higher the older you get. So if you can learn from my mistakes instead of making your own, that's a win-win, right? Wait, how do I win again?

Meh, let's end this introduction of *Independence Day* with a story of me losing (again!)—a story of my Independence Night.

The Graduation All-Night Party

I don't know about you, but I had to work hard to extend my curfew each year I moved up a grade, convincing my parents to agree to 9:00 p.m. on school nights and 10:00 p.m. (sometimes 11:00 p.m. with enough whining) on Fridays and Saturdays. So the night of graduation was my first taste of extreme freedom. We had a city-wide all-night party where the parents and the two city high schools had arranged for different businesses to stay open all night for all the graduates if we had a wristband on. So certain restaurants, bowling alleys, putt-putt golf, even a local lodge turned dance club all coordinated their hours so we had a ton of options for places to celebrate with each other. The freedom the seven hundred of us had, moving in waves across a city of about forty thousand, was awesome. If you saw people driving around at 3:00 a.m. that night, they were most likely some of your classmates.

I had friends ask if I wanted to carpool, but I was so hungry for my freedom that I said, "No way!" I wanted to go where I wanted when I wanted. Even though it was less social, I craved that freedom, especially on that night. It was symbolic! And also symbolic of how I would regularly choose symbolism over fun with my friends. (*Eye roll.*) Seriously, though, with all that freedom, I was pretty scared of all the temptation I would face too. I think I can leave to your imagination all the temptation that can surround a night like that. I went to a large public high school and my graduating class was four

"Independence does not mean solitude. Nothing good grows from an intentional decay into being totally and literally alone."

—Michael DiMarco

hundred. Alcohol, hotel rooms, basically twelve years of semi-controlled angst unleashed. At the time I thought I might become a police officer and was already doing reserve work with my hometown police department, so I avoided those temptations (on that night at least).

But what I remember most about that night is the opportunity. Oh, the opportunity! Hundreds of people who had spent the last four or more years of their lives together, not knowing if we'd ever cross paths again. One of the many destinations that night was an Eagles lodge, one of those men's organizations where guys pay dues to hang out and do, well, I have no idea what they do. I think they just belong to get out of the house and find freedom. But I digress. At the Eagles lodge they set up a dance floor and had a DJ. Sort of a graduation night prom with no dates, tuxedos, or corsages. I made it the last stop on my graduation night crawl, and it was a blast. On one of the last dances of the night, a slow dance, one of my classmates I didn't know very well asked me to dance. During that three-minute song, she basically confessed that she had a long-standing crush for me and couldn't believe that I never noticed. At this point I was totally in shock; I was the class clown and didn't think girls took me seriously, and here was a cheerleader/dance team type giving me a window. I said something lame like "we should go out this summer," but she was leaving in a matter of days and moving out of state. Oh well, just my luck.

Fast forward years later to our high school re-union. She shows up looking exactly the same, cute as ever. After she moved away, it wasn't long until she fell in love, got married to a police officer, and had a bunch of kids and a great life. Exactly what I wanted. Drat! Meanwhile, the smart, funny, good boy who wanted to be a cop and family man at a young age had gotten married and divorced, had no kids of his own, and had even spent time in jail. But that was okay because my life was on the rebound since I was finally learning to deal with freedom, temptation, and opportunity through the mistakes of my life. Yet even with her "good life," this girl still felt the need to ask me a question (twenty years later!): Why did I blow the opportunity that she gave me? The answer was an easy one: *I was stupid.* We laughed and reminisced. She bragged on her kids and I bragged on my dog. We hung out the rest of that night in that ballroom, dancing to music we never thought would be played on an oldies station.

In a time travel setting like a high school reunion, it can be easy to get lost in the past and fall prey to temptation. And on one hand I wanted to. But for one of the first times in my life, I actually handled the temptation instead of the temptation handling (mangling) me. The next morning I flew to a publishing conference where I also met my wife Hayley for what turned out to be a second date. The first date months earlier went awful because I was stupid. Catch a theme here? But I was tired of blowing opportunities, and it was on that second date that we fell in love.

So here I am, a sorta bestselling and award-winning author, married to a very bestselling and award-winning author, telling you how to deal with freedom, temptation, and opportunity. Because you can do it alone, like I did, sometimes learning from your mistakes but needing decades to do it, or you can do it with help, guidance, and experience, especially from the mistakes of others willing to share them! One of the most important things in life is to know that you're not alone. For now, know that I'm with you in the pages of this book. You can learn to leave your fears behind and attack your future independence with confidence because you also have a Father above who loves you and says this:

> Be strong and courageous. Do not fear or be in dread of them, for it is the LORD your God who goes with you. He will not leave you or forsake you.... It is the LORD who goes before you. He will be with you; he will not leave you or forsake you. Do not fear or be dismayed. (Deut. 31:6, 8)

Independent Study

At the end of each chapter, I'm going to ask you a few questions, and I want you to write your answers down in the pages of this book. That way, you can hold on to this book as a little memento of your

Independence Day and have a time capsule of what you were thinking on this day about where you've been, where you are, where you think you're going. Trust me, if you just write down a few short answers to these questions, years from now when you read them your mind will flood your memory with moments from throughout your life that you probably would have never remembered without the scribbles you make in this book. So . . .

What's the thing you're going to miss the least in your life after graduating?

What's the thing you're going to miss the most?

What are you looking forward to the most after graduation?

What do you fear the most about life after graduation?

Freedom

Riding Horses in Kilts

In the movie *Braveheart*, William Wallace gave his ragtag group of Scotsmen a pep talk from atop his horse, urging them on to fight a much larger and more skilled English army. The most famous line of the movie is "They may take our lives, but they will never take our freedom!" And so a bunch of men wearing plaid skirts stood their ground against the superior force and fought the English with ferocity. Then most of the Scots died, and eventually William Wallace was captured, tortured, and beheaded. Now that I think about it, it wasn't really a pep talk. It was a "convince these guys to commit a heroic suicide mission beside me" talk. In kilts. Ah, freedom.

That scene paints a picture of a freedom that has to be fought for. But a skirt-wearing, horse-riding, field-dying freedom is *not* what I think of when I think of graduating. Of course, if you're a girl who rode the bus to school most of your life and gave everything you had during the last game of your senior field hockey season, graduation could be a skirt-wearing, bus-riding, field-"dying" freedom. But if you're not a Scottish highlander or a field hockey player, what does freedom look like to you?

"Freedom lies in being bold."

—Robert Frost

Again, maybe it's easier to start with the opposite of freedom, and that's captivity, confinement, imprisonment, incarceration, limitation, servitude, and slavery. Ugh.

Ever since the beginnings of civilization when slavery was a universal fact of life, freedom has been a cherished part of our best moral fiber. Ancient Scripture, in the book of Exodus, said that Hebrew slaves must be freed by their seventh year of captivity (Exod. 21:2), and in the books of Leviticus and Ezekiel, the Scriptures tell of the Year of Jubilee: every fiftieth year all slaves would be freed and property returned to its owners. So while your life surely shines in comparison to a life of brutal servitude, this time in your life probably feels a little like your Year of Jubilee. After years of living under someone else's (hopefully loving) rule, after years of laboring in the school system (many times against your will), you have been released to pursue life on your terms!

What Is Freedom?

The *New Oxford American Dictionary* defines freedom like this:

1. the power or right to act, speak, or think as one wants without hindrance or restraint
2. the state of not being imprisoned or enslaved

Freedom is the power to do (act, speak, or think) what you want without being told you can't by someone who controls you. In your life right now, today, in this moment and the moments soon to come, freedom means gaining your independence—self-determination, self-rule, and free rein. And it's all an amazing journey you have to take in order for you to become the grown-up you were meant to be. But freedom isn't all cake and ice cream. It isn't all parties and speeches, but it's also responsibility and work. For some it might come with the carry-on of fear or anxiety. For others it might just come with a backpack full of rebellion. However you feel about freedom, what you do with yours will color the rest of your life. Freedom isn't something to fear, but it is something that is more powerful if understood than if misunderstood. Knowledge is power, as the saying goes, so in order to increase your success in life, let's take a look at the first thing you need to know: What does freedom mean in your life, and how do you handle it so that you get the most out of it and waste the least of it? Let's take a quick look at your freedom and what it's going to mean in your life.

The Upside of Freedom

Welcome to the amazing world of a life of freedom. Today you are setting out on your own, making your own way, and taking charge of your own life. Your freedom is your chance to do what you want, when you want. It may be your chance to choose whether you pick up your dirty dishes or leave them till you have nothing left to eat off of. Or it might be your chance to choose where you live, who you live with, and how you decorate. Whatever stage of life you are in, this Independence Day is your chance to do what you want to do without the control or demands of anyone else.

Freedom is something we are all shooting for from the time we are old enough to squirm in our parents' arms. Every human being innately wants the ability to be self-sufficient and self-determined.

To go to the potty on their own, to tie their own shoes, and to make their own way. This is where you've been headed since you were old enough to talk, and there's no stopping it now. Your ultimate freedom has arrived, and whether you feel like it or not, you are ready to take it by the horns. Whether your parents require a tight rein on you even though you've graduated or they've let you loose, you are still stepping into a world of greater freedom than you've ever had. And if you are unwilling to take it as it's given, then you will fail to develop, just like a baby who chooses to crawl for two years rather than to try walking on their own. Independence is inevitable for most human beings and required for growth and success beyond where you are right now. And freedom is a major step into your own independence. To reinforce the great worth that first step has in your life, let's take a look at three major benefits that highlight the tremendous upside of freedom.

Self-Determination

Part of this newfound freedom is the ability to go after your dreams—not the dreams of others but your own dreams, no matter how crazy they are. The beautiful part of freedom is the ability to get to work figuring out what you like to do and how you can do it more often. It's being in charge of your own future, even if it's just your day, your year, your job, or your relationships. You are free to choose them all. And that freedom is a good thing. It's what you exercise when you explore your opportunities and identify your tastes. Self-determination is the ability and the right to make your own path, choose your own road, and climb your own mountain. And it's the opportunity that comes along with your independence, which I'll talk a lot more about in the chapter called (surprisingly) "Opportunity." So stay tuned for that!

Self-Rule

Another amazing benefit of freedom is self-rule—the ability to make up your own to-do list and your own set of rules. When you are a kid living at home, you are under house rules. You don't pay for things, you didn't buy the house, and you aren't old enough to be your own boss, so you live under the authority and rule of your parents. But once that has ended you are free, to some degree, to live life on your own terms. Whether it's deciding whether or not you will go to bed early so you get a good night's sleep or choosing to take all afternoon classes so you can stay up as late as you want, your schedule and the enforcement of it are all up to you.

As a child you needed someone to give you boundaries, to tell you what to do and when to do it. "Don't brush the cat with your toothbrush!" "Don't lick your feet!" All rules set to teach you how to live and how not to live. As you've gotten older, you've learned from those rules and made some of your own. "Don't lick a frozen flagpole." "Never lock your keys in the car." And now it's time to put all your self-determined rules to the test.

Self-rule is a freeing thing because it gives you the ability not only to avoid the punishment of others but also to decide how much work you want to do and how much fun you want to have. Self-rule opens up a world of freedom because it takes the chains off and lets you go at life just the way you want to.

As you explore different ideas and rules for your own life, you will grow and change. You will find that some rules that you inherited from your parents aren't so bad after all, and some are broken and need some fixing. But in everything, self-rule is a part of you growing up and taking your self-discipline and self-control into your own hands, living and learning, failing and succeeding.

Free Rein

Freedom also means having free rein over your life. It means that you are now free to live, to go, to explore, and to learn. When I was twenty, I had the privilege to be able to play volleyball for a men's team that traveled overseas playing various men's national teams but also playing exhibitions for local schools and smaller communities. I had to raise a few thousand dollars to do it, but for someone who had never flown on a plane before, two months, sixteen international flights, and ten full passport pages later, no one felt more independent!

Part of what's amazing about freedom is the ability to experience the world around you. And for you today, the sky's the limit. Sure, there are limitations for all of us, but today is the day when you can decide how hard you want to work to do what it is you want to do. Free rein is the mark of your life now. You are set to make your own way, to decide who you are and who you will become. In this way, you are beginning to define yourself, your faith, and your future. But remember when you learned to ride a bike? You fell down a few times before you got the hang of it. So don't freak out about failure. Today isn't the day you have a perfect life; it's the day you start your new life with its ups and downs, its highs and lows. You might wobble at first, and maybe you even need the training wheels of your parents till you get the hang of things, but with each push of the pedals you get closer and closer to becoming an expert rider.

The Downside of Freedom, aka Freedom Failures

Freedom is meant for every human being, but that doesn't mean that all will take it. Some will see freedom as too much work, as an impossibility, or as something they'll get to when they have some time. Freedom isn't free, as the saying goes. It takes a little bit of participation on your part. Some action is required. So before you take a look at freedom and turn away in fear, let's look at the downside of freedom: a few freedom failures and how to avoid them so that your Independence Day is what the name suggests—a day of progress towards independence rather than regress into more dependence.

"While we are free to choose our actions, we are not free to choose the consequences of our actions."

—Stephen R. Covey

The Victim

True or false: freedom requires the cooperation of those who have authority over you. *False.* While freedom given helps the growth of that freedom, it isn't essential to it. For example, when a parent of an eighteen-year-old living at home says, "I won't pay for Harvard, but I will pay for community college," that might sound oppressive to an honor student who wants an Ivy League education, but in all actuality, that sentence is dripping with freedom. What that sentence is saying is "You're free to choose whatever college you wish" and "You're free to take our money if you go to College X." In fact, you're probably going to meet little resistance to a request to apply the free $3,000 for community college to your $50,000 per year costs for Harvard. You're always free to ask. The big lesson here is to not be enslaved by your situation but see the freedom that is possible within it.

You see, the most helpful thing in life is not the ability to get your way; that's fairy tale freedom. What is truly freeing is to realize that freedom is (remember the dictionary definitions now) your power to act, speak, and think without restraint and to not be imprisoned or enslaved against your will. When you let your parents' $3,000 offer enslave you to think you can never go to Harvard (assuming you have the grades to get in), then you have been imprisoned not by your parents but by your own failure to think outside the box to figure out a way to pay for it yourself. You've handed over your self-determination and independence and become a helpless blob who lets life just happen to you. That's the freedom failure we call being a victim.

Freedom has to do with your thoughts more than your actions, and no one can control your thoughts unless you let them. So freedom starts within. It starts in your mind, with the way you think about the life around you. Slaves living on plantations in pre–Emancipation Proclamation America were anything but free. But they had the freedom to pray and worship God; prayer is impossible for anyone to take away. Every prisoner can find freedom, if not in their actions, at least in their own heart and mind. And the same is true for you. You can find freedom no matter what situation you live in. But that freedom requires something of you: it requires responsibility. In the case of enslavement, it requires the slave to take responsibility for being free within the constraints of their slavery. And it will require the same for you.

So whether your present (or near future) decisions involve the college you're wanting to attend, living at home versus living on your own, or even having the dreaded "stay together or break up" conversation before one of you moves away, all of them have visible and not-so-obvious freedom threads woven throughout the current patch of your tapestry-like life. Don't let victim thinking steal your ability to see freedom in every situation.

The Lazy

Another freedom thief that threatens to keep you under the thumb of control and lost in the abyss of stagnation is laziness. Freedom can be stopped in its tracks by your choice to do absolutely nothing about it. In this scenario the freed one, in this case you, the graduate, is too comfortable with the status quo to risk the unknown future that freedom brings. So the freed one rejects progress and opts for regression, turning away from growth and back to childhood. In these situations graduation signals the end of the memories and ease of being a kid, and the comfort of the known. That's just too much to bear, so the lazy mind determines to get to things later, when it's had time to rest. Potential freedom gets a door slammed in the face, while the only door left open is the one to the apartment over mom and dad's garage. We'll talk more about what the lazy give up in the chapter on opportunity.

The Fearful

Freedom isn't always as effortless or as safe as we'd like it to be. Sometimes freedom is dangerous. It's unknown at best and scary at worst. If fear overcomes you when you think about change, then freedom will make your stomach churn. But letting fear win is becoming a slave to that fear. When you obey something like your fear of danger or the unknown, you give fear authority over your life, and your freedom is gone. But you weren't meant to live in fear, serving it and obeying its every command. You were meant to live in freedom—freedom from all the little gods who try to convince you that the big God who created you can't be trusted with your life. If he can't be trusted, then you should fear, but if he is big enough to protect you and to guide you, then all that fear is useless and should be discarded as such. Don't let fear dictate your life, but trust God and live in the freedom of that trust.

The Isolated

Independence does not mean solitude. Nothing good grows from an intentional decay into being totally and literally alone. You may feel a sense of freedom in shutting yourself off from the world. Locking yourself in your room and playing Xbox or writing in your journal all day might sound like getting away from it all, but when your self becomes your only interaction, then your freedom has been replaced by the prison cell of isolation.

You were made for community, so if you want to live how you were intended to live, then your freedom has to include others. Even if being with others is hard or uncomfortable, it is still a part of being unencumbered with the chains of aloneness. Listen, if you were to meet me at a party, you'd never know that my semi-secret passion is to just be left alone. But when I get my wish, I rarely impact others in a positive way and am never impacted in ways that can come only from others. That's the value of living in community, of being part of something bigger than yourself.

The Truth about Freedom

The truth about freedom is that it doesn't come naturally. Your natural state is bondage or slavery to the things you fear, the things you hate, and the things you run from. That's why freedom requires work. Just like you can't stop cleaning up your house and expect it to stay clean, you can't stop pursuing your freedom and expect to remain free. The natural state of man is the opposite of free. Our natural state is to become a slave to the bad stuff in life—that is, the easy stuff. Stuff like laziness, fear, worry, doubt. All these things try to control you, and it can be super easy to let them. But freedom requires some responsibility on your part. As a glaring example, your freedom demands that you obey the law. If you don't take responsibility and learn the rules of the road, then you might end up getting pulled over and ticketed, or worse, you might end up in jail, where freedom is kept to a minimum. So your freedom is your responsibility. You've got to do the work to get the free. That means stuff like disciplining yourself, since that's no longer anyone else's job but yours, and self-control, which goes a long way to setting you free. When you take responsibility, you grow your own success.

But finding freedom isn't just about you. In fact, one might argue that it's not about you at all but about something much, much greater. See, for a lot of people freedom is about self. It's all about pleasing yourself, doing what you want when you want, and being free to choose without anyone imposing their will on you. The world might tell you that you are not free unless you can do whatever you want whenever you want. But the truth is, when that's the case, then all you are is self-centered and selfish. Making freedom about getting all you can get isn't freedom at all but bondage to your urges and desires. It's really easy to see this in the life of a drug addict. They started taking drugs because they were free to do whatever they wanted, with no one else telling them what to do. So they dove into their freedom with all the passion they could muster. But soon that freedom to do whatever they wanted with their own body became slavery when the very thing they did out of their own independence made them dependent, hooked, addicted.

When your freedom is based on getting what you can get as fast as you can get it, when it's all about meeting your own needs and wants, then you, like the narcissist or third world dictator, are creating a monster of yourself. There is really very little freedom in self because self is never truly satisfied and always demands more—more work, more attention, and more devotion.

Still others find their freedom in other people, looking for what they want and need in the approval of others, as if that will set them free. But this is actually just a twist on living for yourself, like the difference between old-fashioned vanilla and vanilla bean ice cream. And that's because most people live for others because of how it makes them feel. And ultimately, that feeling is still just all about self. When what you do has the goal of serving yourself, then you are in bondage to self. Remember that whoever you serve, you obey. And if pleasing others serves you by making you feel accepted, loved, important, or popular, then self has replaced God on the throne of your life.

The only true freedom is found when you topple all of your little gods with all of their demands on your life and instead find your freedom in the one true God. Thomas Watson said it perfectly when he said, "To serve God, to love God, to enjoy God, is the sweetest freedom in the world." It is freedom because it takes the chains of this world off of your arms and lets you become the person you were meant to become.

Your freedom depends on your faith. If your faith is in yourself, then your freedom will last only as long as your strength. And while your strength may last a while, ultimately it will be reduced by the stuff your self requires in order to be satisfied. As the book of Ecclesiastes says, "The eye never has enough of seeing, nor the ear its fill of hearing" (Eccles. 1:8 NIV). When you try to satisfy yourself over God, you are forever running around, working to please your emotions, your dreams, and your hopes, and forever coming up with failure. But when you put all your energy, all your strength into loving God, then you have all his power and strength, which never end, to give you all you need. Freedom is found in turning your life over to the only One who can handle it. When you do that, your freedom will soar.

Independent Study

What were some memorable moments in your childhood when you felt liberating freedom?

_____

_____

_____

How did you feel and what do you remember about the first time you drove a car alone?

_____

_____

_____

What is the one freedom you're most excited about realizing?

_____

_____

_____

What are the biggest fears you have regarding your newfound freedom?

_____

_____

_____

Temptation

Leaving This Chapter Out Was Tempting

I haven't done a ton of research on graduation books, but I haven't seen any devote much space to the subject of temptation. In fact, the publisher of this book wanted to leave the word out of the subtitle on the cover. They were afraid it was too much of a downer for such an inspirational and positive event. But here's the deal: temptation is a constant in life. If you think you will never be tempted in anything, or at least anything important, then you are setting yourself up for a stumble of epic proportions. Old Bill Shakespeare got that one right; simply being tempted never defines you or your future, but falling prey to what tempts you can and does. Here are three true statements about temptation:

Everyone is tempted.

Everyone falls. (Ever met a perfect person?)

Not everyone falls the same way.

So let me set the scene of my first of many public falls. Throughout my life in high school, I slacked on homework and aced tests. So I'd average a C or

D on homework and get an A or B on my tests for a class grade in the C+ to B- range. All I wanted to do was get through high school with the minimum amount of time allotted to study and busywork, er, homework. And this was all going according to plan until the last semester of my junior year.

All throughout my school career, from first grade to graduation from high school, I was younger and smaller than most everyone in my class because my mom enrolled me in first grade a year early. And while my age never caught up with my classmates' (funny how that works), I eventually got almost all my height by my senior year. I was five foot two when I was a freshman, five eleven going into my senior year, and finally topped out at six two. And because I always felt "behind" in age and size (but not necessarily intelligence), I figured I had two choices:

1. Be the young brainiac freak (I sure made that option sound appealing).
2. Be the comedian, hide my intelligence, and gain acceptance from my "elders."

Because I craved acceptance and affirmation, I chose option 2.

Because of that choice, I basically made the decision in the classroom to concentrate on one-liners instead of lining my notebook with notes. *Disruptive* could've replaced *DiMarco* on my report card. The good news was that most all my teachers enjoyed my humor and only occasionally told me to rein it in. And then there was Mr. Dewitt, my junior year English teacher. Not only did he have a disdain for my humor in class, but he also had a disdain for plagiarism; I had copied whole passages from a study guide for a book I was assigned for my final project. He flunked me, and I had to retake junior English my senior year, this time with the first English teacher that actually "got me," Mr. Shantz. And I was finally with peers my own age. (Yay?)

This was my first public fall of too many in my life. And the falls we experience in succumbing to temptation are definitely the downside to temptation. But before we talk about the ample downside, let me tell you about the upside of temptation.

The Upside of Temptation

Yes, I said it: *there is an upside to temptation*. Scandalous! Who bought you this book and what were they thinking? But before we start burning books and picketing this humble author, check it out: temptation has a huge upside. Temptation can show you who you really are and what is really important in your life. It's like having a teacher who gives pop quizzes the morning after a state championship game, a teacher who secretly hopes that you fail. Yes, you can hate the teacher for that, but if you have studied well and know the subject, the pop quiz just becomes an annoyance at worst and actually engrains your knowledge even deeper. So yes, my independent ones, there is an upside.

Temptation can actually show you your weaknesses and help you to see and strengthen the areas in your life where you not only need to grow but need to make some changes. Facing temptation and not giving in is the way you develop self-control. And self-control is power. As a little kid you had very little self-control (think *diapers*). You did whatever you felt like whenever you felt it. Maybe you were the kind of kid who if you ate something yucky, you would just open your mouth and let it drop out onto

*"'Tis one thing to be tempted,
another thing to fall."*

—William Shakespeare

whatever surface you were standing or sitting over. *Blaak!* Or if you saw someone who looked weird, had an extra arm or something, you would point and yell to your mom, "Why does she look like that?" Little kids lack self-control, mainly because they know so little about not only etiquette but also the benefit of controlling themselves. By now you've hopefully learned a thing or two about self-control and you see some benefit to it. Well, temptation is the training ground for self-control, because self-control is just the ability not to do something that you really want to do. Temptation is not an open invitation to do whatever you want but a mental gym for strength of will and self-awareness. As you resist temptation, you become more in control of your own life, not letting the wind blow and toss you around like a wave on the sea. Temptation, and the act of resisting it, builds you up as you tear down your lack of self-control.

But there is another kind of temptation, different from the expected temptation, and that's the kind of temptation that attempts to pull you away from your natural bent. This is the temptation to do something good, rather than to fall or do something you shouldn't do. For instance, are you overly shy? Well, then occasionally you probably feel tempted to do a silly dance in front of your friends or go up to that girl you really like and ask her out. Okay, maybe just *talk* to her, for a start. But if it's against your natural bent, you probably resist that temptation most days and keep to yourself. Or maybe you've been tempted to speak up and speak out on an injustice you see happening right in front of you, but you resist, and your life stays safe and anonymous because of it.

I once gave in to this kind of temptation when I was at a coffee shop, the kind where you order at the counter. I was sitting at a table by the counter, working on my laptop, when a guy came in and started to order. When the lady repeated his order back to him, she got one thing wrong, and he had a fit. He started yelling at her and cussing her out, and she seemed pretty scared. If he would have just left it at one shout I might have ignored him like the rest of the restaurant. But when he kept on belittling her, I had to speak up. So I said to him, "Just take your bagel and leave her alone." I couldn't resist the temptation to intervene in something that, as he said, was "none of my business." In the end he finally left the server alone and left the restaurant. The women who worked there were so thankful that they still to this day call me their "bouncer" and "hero." That's one temptation I'm proud to say I didn't resist.

So yes, a temptation or pull to do something we don't always do can have an upside. But most temptation, when resisted, has the incredible ability to strengthen your self-control.

The Downside of Temptation

Well, that upside section was short, wasn't it? That's because other than testing your character and drawing out your natural self, temptation is usually there to derail you from your dreams, your goals, and who and what matters most in your life.

Over the course of my life and study, I've come to notice a temptation pattern—a repeated way that temptations come to lure us. Knowing this pattern— having a heads up on the areas in your life where you are going to be tempted—will help turn your downsides into upsides. Chances are, you've already been tempted in one way or another through one of these three areas: appetite, affirmation, and ambition.

Appetite

Let's start with the first and probably most obvious: appetite. This temptation comes in the areas of passion, desire, and hunger. Those things in your life that you love, that make you feel good, that give you relief or comfort are where temptation comes the easiest and the most often. For me this one hits hard in the area of food and comfort. I am easily tempted by food. When I've had a bad day, all I want to do is eat something I call "comfort food." So if we have some salami, some pepperoni, or a box of cookies in the house, then you can bet that's going to be in my belly. Mmm, good and nutritious. Of course, there's nothing wrong with either sweets or meats, in moderation, but this kind of appetite temptation is a hard one to master because of that. Eating isn't a sin; you've got to eat, so why not have another slice (or ten) of pizza? Ah, temptation speaks my language. In this kind of temptation, I most often give in to my desire for the comfort and relief that food promises and (temporarily) delivers.

All temptation comes with a promise. Maybe for you the promise comes in some other form. It might come in your hunger for love or acceptance, for recognition or success. Whatever you crave the most, that's where you're going to be tempted. Knowing what you obsess about, what you think about and want the most, is a good way to prepare yourself for temptations of the appetite.

Before you can fight off any temptation, you have to want to fight it off. So what's the point in fighting off your appetite temptation? You're hungry, for whatever it might be, and that means you have needs that have got to be filled, so what's wrong with filling them? A lot of people would say nothing, but the promises that temptations bring don't always come true. For example, food promises to make me feel better, to comfort me. And while that is true for the fifteen minutes it takes me to eat it, the "gift with purchase" is the extra pounds I tote around and the sugar crash afterward. And every time I give in to my temptation, that temptation owns me even more as it becomes habit. A habit is anything that you do repeatedly, and when it's giving in to a temptation, it's a hard habit to break. That's because the promise of the temptation is so important to us that we just can't let go of giving in to it. We want what it offers, and that's that.

But here's the trouble with appetite temptation: your eyes never get enough of seeing, and your ears never get enough of hearing. That means you become addicted to the sensation that giving in to a temptation rewards you with, but since it's never enough, you keep going back for more. Soon the temptation has you wrapped around its little finger, and when it says, "Jump!" you say, "How high?" This is where the downside to temptation rears its ugly face—when it controls you. At this point temptation becomes your master and you its slave. And breaking free becomes a lifelong battle.

Appetite is more than just a craving for food. It can be the desire for sex, material possessions, or basically anything else you can consume and still feel the need for more. Even eating disorders are in the appetite arena; they feed your insatiable appetite for control. And so appetite is rarely satisfied and therefore rarely gives up asking for more.

Self-control becomes the only way out from under its control.

Affirmation

Now let's look at the second pattern of temptation, and that's affirmation. Affirmation is about being accepted or noticed. It's about being thought of, being looked at, and being followed. Affirmation offers the sensation of acceptance, something every one of us craves. And because of that we can easily be tempted to do things that aren't good for us because they promise us affirmation.

I've given in to the affirmation temptation hundreds of times in my life. That's because for most of my life, I've craved pleasing people so much. In fact, if I can't please people, then I feel like a failure. So for most of my life I've done stupid things, crazy things, in order to make other people happy, even when

*"Some temptations come
to the industrious, but all
temptations attack the idle."*

—Charles Spurgeon

those same things would ultimately make my life miserable. But my desire to please others trumped my desire to please myself when temptation came. In a weird twist of events, I would want to feel good, and in order to feel good, I would have to please others, but pleasing them made me feel bad, so the feel-good sensation I wanted never materialized. Ugh, what a treadmill to nowhere.

This is the perfect picture of the fake promises of temptation. They promise so much and deliver so little. In fact, most temptation delivers more pain than good in the end. And that's the biggest downside to temptation: it doesn't pay off what it promises. Temptation is a liar.

Affirmation plays on your need for love; it plays on your need to feel important and special. That's why so many people are obsessed with how many Facebook friends or Twitter followers they have.

And ultimately it plays upon your pride, your sense that you deserve affirmation, and so you're going to get that affirmation however you can. And you know what they say about pride, right? It comes before the fall. Any choice that you make based on pride—on thinking you should get what you want when you want it—sets your desire up as a little god that needs to be catered to and honored no matter what the cost.

I can tell you from experience that affirmation temptations can ruin your life, or at least make you feel that way until you learn to combat them.

Ambition

The third way that temptation comes is by whispering promises in your ear that tickle your desire for more power and achievement. Ambition is something you've probably spent a bit of time thinking about and planning for as of late. And while wanting more out of life isn't inherently bad (it's actually important as you step out into your new life), just like with appetite and affirmation, ambition temptation takes something that can help you and turns it into something that can consume you.

Ambition can make people do some crazy things. It can end friendships, destroy marriages, and even start wars. The temptations that play on your ambition will ask you to do some things that are inconsistent with who you are and who you want to become. Like I said, wanting more in life isn't all bad, but when you want more and are willing to go after it at the expense of everything and everyone else, then temptation has had its way with you. You are an easy target when ambition is your god, when you live to serve it and do whatever it takes to get it. There is a big misconception about the idea of money and faith. A lot of people think the Bible says that money is the root of all evil. But that's not exactly true. There are two more very important words in that verse that change its entire meaning, and they are the words *love* and *of*. It is the *love of money* that is the root of all kinds of evil, not the money itself (see 1 Tim. 6:10).

Ambition temptations, just like the appetite and affirmation ones, play upon your particular loves. They promise more of what you love, so if what you love is money or power, they will promise you more than you could ever imagine. And just like any other kind of temptation, the ambition kind insists that what you want is the most important thing in the world and you've got to have it no matter what the cost. This is where temptation strikes a nerve—in the area of expectation. When you expect more for yourself, and especially when you insist upon it, then self-control takes a backseat to feeding your ambition.

Another major temptation that surrounds ambition is avoiding all ambition at all costs. Whether it's wanting to avoid success or just the work associated with success, in this kind of temptation, there is a strong fear of either failure or effort. Fear, disguised as laziness, tells the fearful that to want more, to push, to drive, is to ensure failure. And like most lies, this one is cloaked in the truth. *Failure is a certainty in life.* We will all fail at some point or another. But the one who refuses to try fails 100 percent of the time, while the one who at least tries will eventually succeed, and so failure hits them less than 100 percent of the time. And since you've graduated, I know you haven't failed math, so you know that less than 100 percent failure is better than the maximum.

In this negative way of thinking about ambition, the downside to temptation is that when tempted to succeed in healthy ways, like getting a good job, moving out of your parents' basement, and falling in love, you are tempted too much by your fear of failure to make forward progress into independence. I'll talk more about this in the final chapter.

Let me just say that ambition is not a sin. Wanting to succeed is okay, but wanting more than you need is suspect. When ambition pushes you to do things you wouldn't ordinarily do, or when it just flat out pushes you to sin, then you've come face-to-face with the downside of temptation and kissed it on the lips.

Rejecting Temptation's Advances

Your temptation is nothing new. It's been going on since the very first people walked the face of the earth, and it has come to every person since then. No one is exempt. In fact, not even Jesus, the Son of God, was exempt from temptation's attacks. Immediately after Jesus was baptized by his cousin John in the Jordan River, he was taken by the Holy Spirit out into the wilderness with the sole purpose of being tempted by the devil. After fasting for forty days, Jesus was weak, and the devil came to him offering him three things: food for his *appetite*, *affirmation* of who he was (the Son of God), and the *ambition* of having all the earth admire his glory. But all of these cravings Jesus rejected. In his perfection he knew that none of this would give him what it seemed to promise. In fact, all the temptations promised were lies—untruths stretched to look better than they were. And to every false promise Jesus responded with a promise that would ring true for eternity. He responded with God's promises, and with those he defeated not only temptation but the tempter. (For more on this, turn to "How to Resist Temptation" on page 120 and see Matthew 4:1–11.)

Temptation promises more than it ever gives. As you gain more and more independence, you will be tempted more and more to do things that make great promises to your appetite, need for affirmation, and ambition. How you respond to those temptations will shape your destiny. Your temptation isn't anybody else's responsibility. And the truth is, you will never be tempted beyond what you can bear, and this is something common to every human being on earth (see 1 Cor. 10:13). In other words, you are not alone! Temptation is a normal part of life, but it's what you do with it that can make you abnormal. Going with the flow of temptation is the easy part; resisting it for something far greater, far more valuable, is hard work. But hard work pays off in the form of a greater independence and opportunities for the future. When temptation wins and you give in, your independence gets eaten up, devoured by your appetite for more. What once was freedom and independence becomes bondage and dependence. Don't let temptation fool you—it has its value and its dangers. When you know the difference and you are prepared for the temptations that are sure to come, then your future will be yours to live and to thrive in.

Independent Study

Now's the chance for you to do some soul searching on the topic of temptation. Take a look at your heart, mind, and life so far.

What is your greatest personal temptation in the area of

- appetite?

_____

_____

- affirmation?

_____

_____

- ambition?

_____

_____

Do you have someone in your life you can go
   to or call on when you are tempted? Who is
   it? If not, who is someone you can ask to be
   that person?

_____

_____

_____

_____

Opportunity

My six-year-old daughter's favorite (okay, it's really my favorite) knock-knock joke is:

Me: Knock, knock.

You: Who's there?

Me: Interrupting Cow.

You: Interrupting . . .

Me: Moo.

Most everyone has heard the phrase, "opportunity knocks." It basically means that opportunities will not let themselves into your life on their own. They'll let you know that they're there, but you've got to get off the couch to let opportunity in or turn down your music to hear it knocking. But that's only part of the story, only part of the saying. The whole old English proverb is "opportunity knocks *but once*." Now the saying has increased urgency; you get only one chance to seize opportunity (or at least each unique opportunity).

Who knows how many opportunities you've left unanswered because you were blasting headphones or had shampoo in your hair? Or simply because you were just too afraid to answer the door? Maybe you were like me and you underperformed in high school and wasted opportunities for scholarships. Or maybe your lost opportunities revolve around relationships—friends, family, or romantic ones. Whatever unanswered opportunities you mourn, here is the most important thing for you to grasp and remember:

> More opportunities will come. *Different ones*, but more will come.

In fact, your Independence Day is your declaration that you now take full responsibility for being prepared to answer the door. You see, it's not just kids who let others (parents and teachers) look out for their future opportunities. Adults do it all the time; any human being can abdicate door-answering responsibilities to another human being in their life, like a girlfriend/boyfriend, spouse, or boss. But you can also give up opportunity to simple but paralyzing fear. So to best take advantage of your newfound independence, let's take a look at both the upside and downside of opportunity.

The Upside of Opportunity

Opportunity is just a chance to do something. Usually we think of it as a chance to do something good. Of course, in the area of temptation, it might be the chance to do something bad, but hey, that was the last chapter. Now we are talking about the chance to make your dreams come true, to strike out and explore the world, to fall down and get back up again. Opportunity awaits, and all you have to do is take it.

You will never have more opportunities in front of you than today. Each day that passes, so does that day's opportunity. So look at today as the first day of the rest of your chances to do something, or, as they all say, the first day of the rest of your life. Up until now your opportunities have probably been limited by your dependence on parents or teachers. And that was good for a time, but now that you are moving into independence, you are no longer limited by those who were making your choices for you. Sure, there are limitations like laws, money, and time, but opportunity is still at its ripest at this time in your life.

You Can Build on It

One of the biggest upsides of opportunity is the foundation it can give to your dreams. When you first graduate, people say things like "the sky's the limit" and "reach for the stars." They talk about how you can do and be anything you want to do and be if you just go for it. And while all that may be true, the greater truth is that opportunities are built one upon the other. It's a delusion to think that opportunity means one chance to do one big thing and to quickly "make it big." This way of thinking about opportunity is more defeating than uplifting. "Anyone can be president!" is a crock, because in the history of the United States, fewer than fifty men (and no women) have filled that position. A big lottery ticket of an opportunity comes as often as Powerball jackpot numbers do. The best way of looking at it is that each opportunity, if taken full advantage of, is another block in the foundation of your success.

It's really easy to look at an "overnight" success and think they were just in the right place at the right time, but the truth is, the overnight success is one in a million. For most people their success wasn't overnight; it just exploded out of nowhere after years and years of lots of other smaller opportunities seized.

So don't freak out when the opportunities in front of you aren't super amazing. They don't need to be. You don't have to wait for your big shot to

*"Luck is what happens
when preparation
meets opportunity."*

—Seneca

become a big shot; you just have to take advantage of the opportunities that come your way, no matter how small.

You Can Make a Change

It shouldn't be hard to see that change is another upside to opportunity, no matter how small it is. Opportunity is simply another knock on the door. It might open to someplace you never even dreamed of going or it might be the very path you've been pursuing for years, but as soon as you open the door, it's a gateway into change. When you step through a door, you move from one space to another, and for most people this means progress. Even if you're just going from the house to the garage, it's still progress to being on your way. And progress is essential for success.

Think about your dreams for a second. In order for them to come true, you have to get up and get going. Dreams don't become reality until you get out of bed and get moving. As you do that, doors start to open up and opportunities begin to show themselves. And that's when you find another upside to opportunity: the chance to move, to grow, to change.

Without the opportunity to move, grow, or change, there would be no chance for success. Failure is simply the refusal to take the opportunities given to you. For example, a guy would be considered a failure if he was the son of a really rich man and had everything he ever wanted, but he spent every day playing video games alone in his room (sounds like an Adam Sandler movie). This guy may have everything he ever needs and be able to do whatever he wants, but his life is a failure because he never looks for or takes the opportunity that is swirling around him. If he did, then his life would be moving, progressing, and improving, not staying the same.

Opportunity gets you one step closer to your dreams as it changes the status quo. If that's a scary thing for you, think about it like this: If you keep doing what you're doing and don't seize those opportunities, you'll keep getting what you've got. Is that enough? If the status quo is enough for you, then opportunity means very little, but if you are looking for more, if your dreams exceed your reality, then it's time to start looking for the open door of opportunity. What change is waiting on the other side?

Change Your Finances

One thing opportunity gives you a chance to change is your financial future. A lot of people have more outgo than income. They struggle to make ends meet, to get out of debt, and to save themselves from financial failure. But the beauty of the opportunity coming your way is that it can give you the chance to increase your income-making potential. As I said earlier, money isn't evil, and neither is the desire to have enough to live without depending on others to help you out. Over your lifetime you will have lots of opportunities, and whether you take the ones that lead to financial health or financial ruin is up to you. But no matter which comes your way, you can be sure that more opportunity awaits at every step of your future.

The well-known financial advisor Dave Ramsey knows much of opportunity and financial success, but he also knows much of financial failure. Ramsey is a *New York Times* bestselling author of several books on financial wisdom and a syndicated talk show host. But that wasn't always the case. Many years ago Ramsey was in financial ruin, to the point of bankruptcy. But he didn't let that define his life. Instead he seized all the opportunity he could to get back onto his feet. He took the opportunity to stop using debt to fund a pursuit of wealth and started a movement to help people live on less than they make and to live debt-free. That movement, starting in his own life, changed not only his family tree but also the family trees of people all over the world. Was it one big opportunity that got him out of debt and into success? No, it was taking a series of opportunities, or "baby steps," that built the foundation to his "overnight" mega-success today.

The same can be true for you. You can change your financial status by looking at opportunities, both big and small, as they come to you and determining to build a stable foundation of opportunity rather than wait for one big lotto chance to get rich in an instant.

*"Opportunity is missed by most
people because it is dressed in
overalls and looks like work."*

—Thomas Edison

Change Your Family Tree

Opportunity is also your chance to change your family tree. Today, as you take your independence, you begin to become a change agent for your future. Up until now you may have been restricted by things in your life brought about by the limitations of your heritage. You may come from a poor family, a bad family, a weird family, or an underachieving family, but that doesn't mean things have to stay the same. Today isn't just the first day of the rest of your life; it's the first day of the rest of your family legacy. As you seize the opportunities that lead to growth and maturity, you begin to affect not only yourself but also all those who will come after you.

I was raised in a dysfunctional family, to say the least. I am the youngest of six children, spread almost twenty years apart from oldest to youngest, and I have virtually no contact with any of them.

My family was raised, I think accidentally, to distrust one another and to hold grudges. Pitted against one another from an early age, we never learned the truth about life and love but only about survival of the fittest. Instead of being a close-knit family with great memories and loving moments, we were a collection of isolationists and doubters. And while I love my family, as I attempt to make contact with people I haven't seen in decades, I find that we aren't much of a family at all.

But now I have the opportunity to change my bloodline (which rests, by the way, solely in my hands, as none of my five siblings have had any kids of their own except one adopted son). The opportunity to change the family dynamic by teaching my child grace, forgiveness, and love is the chance to change my family tree and to build a loving family—one where we aren't so easily wounded and one that is a place of healing instead of a place of hurt.

If your family isn't the dream family, all is not lost. Today is your opportunity to begin to work the change you need in your life so that when it's time to create your own family, it will be an improvement on the family tree.

In the beginning God planted the very first family tree in the Garden of Eden, and now it's your chance to imitate the Creator. Opportunity is the chance to take on the very creative nature of God and to form your life anew. All that has happened in your past is all that had to happen to get you to today, but now is the time to create something new, to envision your future and walk through the doors that align with that future. Opportunity is your chance to create. And every choice you make creates a part of the rest of your life.

Change Your World

But not only is opportunity the chance to change your future and your family tree, it's also the chance to change the world. Changing the world sounds like something you might hear at a Miss America pageant. It might sound ridiculously lame, but the world changes all the time, and it changes because of the people who live in it, and you are one of those people. Life on this planet can change in an instant, and it can change at the hands of very few people. And you are one of those people.

At the end of your life, will you be able to say that your existence made any difference? Are people better off for having known you? Is the world better off for having housed you? As you hear opportunity knock and answer it, you become a part of history. And while you may never make the history books, you will make the history of at least a few dozen people who will never forget you. You may even find yourself writing a few books! Opportunity is the repeated and varied chance to leave your mark. But if you shy away from opportunity and insist that change is too frightening or too difficult, then your mark will be significantly smaller than it could be. Today, your Independence Day, is your chance to shape the way your future is remembered.

The Downside of Opportunity

It isn't hard to see the upside of opportunity; up is opportunity's very nature. And for most people it isn't the lack of trying but the apparent lack of opportunity that brings them down. But opportunity does have its downsides, and the biggest one is the "opportunity" to fail. Every time you attempt something, there is a chance you won't succeed,

*"I will prepare and some day
my chance will come."*

—Abraham Lincoln

and that's a game changer (or ender) for a lot of people. But failure is meant not to derail you but to redirect you. Failure is a natural part of life; there is no human being on earth who hasn't failed and won't fail again in the future. *You should expect failure.* However, it's not the failure itself but what you do with the failure that matters. Thomas Edison failed thousands of times before he invented the lightbulb. Of that failure he said, "I have not failed. I've just found ten thousand ways that won't work." It might take you ten thousand attempts to succeed, but success will never come if you consider failure to be a controlling factor in your life.

Opportunity is messy. Like the artist who works hard on her painting, spilling paint as she lifts brush to canvas, so is the person who takes the opportunity to change his or her life. Change is messy; creation is messy; it requires many moving parts, and those moving parts can displace the order of things. But messy isn't always bad when it's mess with a reason. When the artist sits down to create, she isn't attacking her work without any rhyme or reason, but she has prepared and worked hard to get herself where she is. Opportunity is the same way; it requires preparation and hard work. To think that opportunity is a free ride to stardom or riches is to believe a lie. Opportunity requires something of you. *It requires a lot from you.*

First of all, it requires preparation. If I had the opportunity to get a record deal tomorrow, it would be an opportunity lost because I have not spent the time that I would need to have spent working on my singing voice in order to make that opportunity pay off. Now, if I were given a shot to write for *The Daily Show* or *Saturday Night Live* tomorrow, that's an opportunity I might just succeed at, because I've honed my writing and comedic skills for so long. So useful, my efforts! Whatever the skill or knowledge, preparation increases your chance at success. You can't be so naïve as to think that all you need in life is a chance—that's only half of it. Preparation is the other half.

But opportunity also requires hard work. When I got the opportunity to be a head volleyball coach at the university level in my late twenties, it was because I had worked hard to make myself known by the athletic department staff and make myself indispensable so that when the position did become open, I was the natural choice.

Opportunity is often built on hard work. If you are afraid of the work, then the opportunity, even if it should knock, won't last long. And while hard work can be called a downside to opportunity, it's also responsible for much of it. So it can't be ignored or dismissed as too much trouble.

Another big downside of opportunity comes when your goals and dreams, your search for opportunity, become your obsession. While opportunity is good, it isn't God, and to obsess over it all the time by giving it all of your heart, soul, mind, and strength is to make it an idol, a little god that you worship and cater to 24-7. Opportunity is desirable, but it's dangerous when valued above preparation, hard work, and devotion.

You know your dream has gotten out of control when you have decided that you will do whatever it takes to get what you want. When no moral standard, no wisdom, no law is beyond stepping on to get what you want, then your dreams have become your god. When you will compromise your faith and your values to achieve your goals, something is out of whack. And danger is on its way.

You know your dreams are out of control when you spend more time thinking about them than about the people around you. When all your thoughts and all your energy are spent on thinking about yourself, then you are unable to love others because you're so in love with your dreams that there's no room for anyone else. In fact, others can become a roadblock, diversion, and distraction in the pursuit of your goals. At this point opportunity takes a turn for the worse as it just adds more fuel to the fire of your passions. Passion isn't a bad thing; it's another one of those essential things. It just gets bad when it's your reason for living, the sole focus of your soul, your object of worship. Your passion doesn't deserve your worship. Only one

God deserves that, and to put anything or anyone else in that position is to set a course for disaster.

Passion, in order to be healthy, can't be inward directed but needs to be outward and upward directed. Passion is the fuel of your dreams when your passion rests not on your success or failure but on your belief in the One who brings your success or failure, all for his own glory. Opportunity, when looked at in this light, is never to be feared but is to be embraced as the chance to see what God is going to do next for the furthering of his kingdom. When God and God alone is your number one goal, then your success is assured, because God never fails.

Your life will *never* be considered a failure as long as it is lived in the pursuit of God. When that's your goal, every opportunity you seize will be maximized to its highest potential—and if failure is its highest potential, even that will be used for good (see

Rom. 8:28). If you believe in a God who knows all, sees all, and is everywhere at once, then you have to know that *the world is your opportunity*. And that opportunity is not to be feared but to be embraced. Today is the first day of your unlimited opportunity to love God and love others. What will you do?

Independent Study

What is one opportunity that you feel you have missed, and why didn't you seize it?

What areas of your life do you need to work on to prepare for your big moment of future opportunity?

_____

_____

_____

_____

What is one goal or opportunity that you've been hoping for a "lottery" answer to but need to approach with "baby steps"?

_____

_____

_____

_____

Knowledge
Is Independence

On this, your Independence Day, you are moving out into a new world of freedom, temptation, and opportunity. This is a world that every human being is asked to enter in order to establish their way in this life, but not all of us handle independence as well as we could.

If you haven't figured it out by now, this book isn't just about you, but it's also an introduction to the One who created you. So if you're not interested in reading about the mechanism behind how what I've been talking about works, stop reading right here. With the disclaimer that it's not really about me either, I'm going to tell you how I figured this all out—or better yet, who helped me to figure this all out—because through this knowledge, you can gain the independence I've got.

How to Gain Your Freedom

Freedom, though promised by many a constitution, is an elusive thing. Many claim they have it, but very few actually do. The truth, in the words of that famous philosopher-musician Bob Dylan, is "No one is free! Even the birds are chained to the sky." A lot

*"Knowledge is indispensable
to Christian life and service.
If we do not use the mind
that God has given us,
we condemn ourselves to
spiritual superficiality and
cut ourselves off from many
of the riches of God's grace."*

—John Stott

of so-called free people are actually living in secret bondage, one they themselves aren't even aware of. The bondage of their dreams, their passions, their wants, and even their needs controls them, and so their freedom is only an illusion.

When what you want is peace, hope, love, protection, forgiveness, compassion, and relationship, and you look in the wrong place for these things, then you end up in bondage to the object of your desire. It's like this: When you look to success to keep you warm, safe, and happy, and success fails you, then where do you turn? When your desire for success asks you to walk away from those who love you, what do you do? When your passion gets in the way of peace and contentment, your freedom to do whatever you want doesn't feel so free anymore.

Freedom is less about doing whatever you want whenever you want to and more about having the strength of spirit and will to say no to those things that threaten to enslave you, those things that make you great promises but in the end demand more of you than you are capable of giving. There is a freedom that is eternal, perfect, and complete. This is the freedom that chains the birds to the sky. It's not the fake freedom that you get from your attempts to live life on your own terms but the freedom that comes from living your life the way it was designed to be lived. Of course I'm talking about the freedom that comes from God, the one who made this life of freedom possible.

The book of Galatians says, "For freedom Christ has set us free; stand firm therefore, and do not submit again to a yoke of slavery" (5:1). The yoke of slavery is bondage to the things that control you,

things like your need to be loved or to have money, things that you can't get out of your head, addiction, unforgiveness, and regret. These are yokes of slavery that threaten to crush you. But when you turn your life over to the love of Jesus, you are set free. As it says in Romans 6:18, you, "having been set free from sin, have become slaves of righteousness." It is a far better thing (in fact, the only good thing) to be a slave to righteousness, which means being a slave to what is right, than to be a slave to the poisonous things that want to control you. In bird talk, it's like being either chained to the sky or chained to the sludge of an oil spill. One allows you to fly with virtually limitless abandon; the other soaks your body in a toxic and grounding mess.

The success of your Independence Day rests on your ability, or rather desire, to live free from bondage to all addictions and obsessions and to live life to the full as it was meant to be lived. One of the most important verses in the Bible says this: "If you declare that Jesus is Lord, and believe that God brought him back to life, you will be saved" (Rom. 10:9 GW). What you are saved from is sin, and that means you don't have to stay in the bondage that threatens to destroy you; that means you are set free. Free to live, to love, to laugh; free to be just who you were meant to be. Jesus said that he came to give you life to the full (see John 10:10), and freedom is an essential part of that life to the full. With this life comes the single most important gift of God, and that is this: "Those who are believers in Christ Jesus can no longer be condemned" (Rom. 8:1 GW). Freedom from condemnation is the most freeing freedom there is! You are not doomed anymore; you are not a victim; you are not helpless or hopeless but free—free to take life by the horns, free to risk, free to soar. When you put all your thoughts, all your hopes, all your energy into loving and serving God, then freedom is instantly yours, no matter what chains you may be wearing.

Your freedom is ripe for the taking. All you have to do is determine to stop living for your own dreams and desires and to start living for the One who created the sky. With the help of his own Spirit, you are free to live life to the full.

How to Resist Temptation

Temptation is a part of the human condition. And while Jesus is God, he is not oblivious to the pull of temptation, because he experienced the human condition while here on earth. The temptation of Jesus that you see in the Gospels is there as a vivid and proven example of how to resist temptation. As I said earlier, Jesus was tempted with appetite, affirmation, and ambition. And his only weapon against these was something called the sword of the Spirit, or the Word of God (see Eph. 6:17). Let's look at how Jesus used passages of Scripture against each of the three temptations:

Appetite

Then Jesus was led up by the Spirit into the wilderness to be tempted by the devil. And after fasting forty days and forty nights, he was hungry. And the tempter came and said to him, "If you are the Son of God, command these stones to become loaves of bread." But he answered, "It is written,

"'Man shall not live by bread alone,
    but by every word that comes
    from the mouth of God.'"

Affirmation

Then the devil took him to the holy city and set him on the pinnacle of the temple and said to him, "If you are the Son of God, throw yourself down, for it is written,

> "'He will command his angels
>   concerning you,'

and

> "'On their hands they will bear you
>   up,
> lest you strike your foot against a
>   stone.'"

Jesus said to him, "Again it is written, 'You shall not put the Lord your God to the test.'"

Ambition

Again, the devil took him to a very high mountain and showed him all the kingdoms of the world and their glory. And he said to him, "All these I will give you, if you will fall down and worship me." Then Jesus said to him, "Be gone, Satan! For it is written,

> "'You shall worship the Lord your God
> and him only shall you serve.'"

Then the devil left him, and behold, angels came and were ministering to him.

Matthew 4:1–11

Think about the ways you've been tempted in the past and how you tried to overcome the temptation, if you even tried. How did you do it? And how did it work for you? Temptation is a big challenge because it offers so much of what you love, but to defeat the lie that what you love will complete you, the truth is the best weapon ever!

When it comes to your appetite for more—how you never get enough of what you love—how do you handle yourself so that you don't end up addicted, obsessed, or enslaved to the very thing you went after? Remember these words and see if they don't help:

> Now there is great gain in godliness with contentment, for we brought nothing into the world, and we cannot take anything out of the world. But if we have food and clothing, with these we will be content. (1 Tim. 6:6–8)

And these words of Jesus are a good reminder but also a good weapon when more is looking delicious, whatever more may be:

> Be careful to guard yourselves from every kind of greed. Life is not about having a lot of material possessions. (Luke 12:15 GW)

*"Faith holds on to
truth and reason from
what it knows to be fact."*

—Martyn Lloyd-Jones

When you can look at your life this way—as dependent not on what you own but on what you do, who you love, and how you are loved—then you are free from bondage and the power of temptation to derail you from success and hope. The only person who isn't content is the person who never gets enough. When just what you have is enough for you, then you will find that you always have just what you need. Contentment leads to happiness because contentment satisfies and relieves the strain and struggle of accumulation. Remember, you can't take any of it with you, except the memory of the lives you have touched and the difference you have made.

But what about the area of affirmation? If you struggle with wanting to fit in, to be accepted, and to be thought well of, even if it means you have to do the wrong things, then have I got a weapon for you. This is one of the most important weapons in my arsenal against my desire to be a people pleaser and to go after their affirmation over anything else; it's from Galatians 1:10 and it goes like this:

> For am I now seeking the approval of man, or of God? Or am I trying to please man? If I were still trying to please man, I would not be a servant of Christ.

It is a good thing to care about others, to want to do things for them, to love them, and to serve them, but when you live for their affirmation of how well you did or how good you are, then your freedom has gone out the window and temptation has lured you into the bondage of people pleasing. But God's words are priceless in the fight against this kind of stuff. Learn them, love them, and use them!

When it comes to ambition, the temptation is to push on no matter what the costs so that you can reach your dreams. But dreams that are made by your selfishness, disregard for others, or need for the approval of others are broken dreams. One of the most important things I've learned about life is the law of pride and humility. And Jesus's command to love my neighbor as myself (see Matt. 22:39) cuts to the heart of my pride. In John Piper's book *What Jesus Demands from the World*, Piper addresses this command to love this way: "It is a very radical command. It cuts to the root of sin called pride—the passion to be happy (self-love) contaminated and corrupted by two things: (1) the unwillingness to see God as the only fountain of true and lasting joy, and (2) the unwillingness to see other people as designed by God to receive our joy in him."[1]

Pride is the foundation of all sin. It was the reason for the original sin of Satan and Adam and Eve. It was

1. John Piper, *What Jesus Demands from the World* (Wheaton: Crossway Books, 2006), 264.

the source behind the sins of Pharaoh, David, Saul, and everyone after them. Pride brings destruction. In this big flip of what the world thinks is the truth, Jesus says, "Those who honor themselves will be humbled, but people who humble themselves will be honored" (Luke 14:11 GW). In other words, operate out of your pride and you'll find humiliation. But operate out of your humility and God will bring you honor.

Your pride makes a lot of demands and sometimes enforces a lot of punishments for failure. It can make you hate yourself, withdraw from the world, and give up on it all just as quickly as it can make you put everyone else down and make yourself the most important person in the world. That's because pride is all about you—your best and your worst. It makes you the star of the show, while humility makes Jesus the star of the show. When the latter is the case, everything runs as planned and you're content because you know that life is not about what you do but about what God is doing through you.

In the battle against temptation, not only do you have one who understands you in the person of Jesus, but you aren't alone. Everyone in the world is tempted just as much, and the Holy Spirit who is within you helps you to overcome each temptation. So don't let temptation convince you that all is lost, when all is actually gained.

How to Seize Opportunity

One of the hardest things about opportunity is knowing which one is a good one and which one isn't. A lot of believers talk about the will of God and how to know what that is. They agonize over what to do and if it's God's will or not, and they ultimately become paralyzed by the fact that they can't clearly hear the voice of God tell them what decisions to make. Well, let's put an end to that right now. The best way to make a decision is to think about your choices like this: You have been given a big playground to play on. And God doesn't care where you play as long as you stay on the playground. You can play on the teeter-totter or the slide, the swings or the monkey bars; just stay on the playground.

Is what you want to do a sin? Is there a verse against it in Scripture? What do other wise men and women of God have to say about it? If you've taken these questions into account, choose away, and know that whatever you choose will be God's will. The Bible confirms that "The heart of man plans his way, but the LORD establishes his steps" (Prov. 16:9). So don't let yourself get paralyzed over making the perfect decision when choosing

between two perfectly good things. Choose what you like and allow God to determine your steps.

Independence Day—CliffsNotes Style

In tribute to my old English teachers Mr. Dewitt and Mr. Shantz, here's the gist of what you've just read over the course of this book, CliffsNotes style. Your Independence Day is the start of a new chapter in your life, which gives you an opportunity to decide who you are going to serve. You can be self-serving, you can serve others (which is kind of like serving yourself as well), or you can serve the One who created you. Regardless of who you serve, along the way you're going be tempted in three ways: through appetite, affirmation, and ambition. Being tempted is something you can't avoid; even the Son of God had to endure it. His model of response using Scripture is our blueprint for resisting temptation. How you respond to those temptations is going to weigh heavily on the opportunities that come your way. But ignoring opportunity out of laziness, through lack of preparation, or because of just plain fearfulness only injures you and keeps you from changing your family tree and the world around you.

My hope is that you scribble in this book, keep it, and use it when you find that you're face-to-face with moments of freedom, temptation, and opportunity in your life. To help you further, I've included a list of Quick Relief verses in the back of the book that you can go to when searching for help navigating this brave new world of independence in your life. Not only do you have this book, but you've also got me and my wife, Hayley, to coach you along the way at Godguy.com and Godgirl

.com (I'm at the guy one). We'd love for you to stop by and hang out with the rest of us who are still learning to live outside the nest and are happily chained to the sky.

Happy Independence Day!

Quick Relief

*Verses to Guide You through Freedom,
Temptation, and Opportunity*

Freedom

> The LORD is on my side; I will not fear.
> What can man do to me? (Ps. 118:6)

> We know that our old self was crucified with him in
> order that the body of sin might be brought to nothing,
> so that we would no longer be enslaved to sin. For one
> who has died has been set free from sin. (Rom. 6:6–7)

There is therefore now no condemnation for those who are in Christ Jesus. (Rom. 8:1)

So, whether you eat or drink, or whatever you do, do all to the glory of God. (1 Cor. 10:31)

For am I now seeking the approval of man, or of God? Or am I trying to please man? If I were still trying to please man, I would not be a servant of Christ. (Gal. 1:10)

For freedom Christ has set us free; stand firm therefore, and do not submit again to a yoke of slavery. (Gal. 5:1)

For you were called to freedom, brothers. Only do not use your freedom as an opportunity for the flesh, but through love serve one another. (Gal 5:13)

Temptation

You shall not covet your neighbor's house; you shall not covet your neighbor's wife, or his male servant, or his female servant, or his ox, or his donkey, or anything that is your neighbor's. (Exod. 20:17)

> Better is the little that the righteous has
>> than the abundance of many wicked.
>> (Ps. 37:16)

He who loves money will not be satisfied with money, nor he who loves wealth with his income; this also is vanity. (Eccles. 5:10)

For where your treasure is, there your heart will be also. (Matt. 6:21)

No one can serve two masters, for either he will hate the one and love the other, or he will be devoted to the one and despise the other. You cannot serve God and money. Therefore I tell you, do not be anxious about your life, what you will eat or what you will drink, nor about your body, what you will put on. Is not life more than food, and the body more than clothing? ... But seek first the kingdom of God and his righteousness, and all these things will be added to you. (Matt. 6:24–25, 33)

No temptation has overtaken you that is not common to man. God is faithful, and he will not let you be tempted beyond your ability, but with the temptation he will also provide the way of escape, that you may be able to endure it. (1 Cor. 10:13)

Am I saying this now to win the approval of people or God? Am I trying to please people? If I were still trying to please people, I would not be Christ's servant. (Gal. 1:10 GW)

Do all things without grumbling or questioning, that you may be blameless and innocent, children of God without blemish in the midst of a crooked and twisted generation, among whom you shine as lights in the world. (Phil. 2:14–15)

Finally brothers, whatever is true, whatever is honorable, whatever is just, whatever is pure, whatever is lovely, whatever is commendable, if there is any excellence, if there is anything worthy of praise, think about these things. What you have learned and received and heard and seen in me—practice these things, and the God of peace will be with you. (Phil. 4:8–9)

Do not love the world or the things in the world. If anyone loves the world, the love of the Father is not in him. For all that is in the world—the desires of the flesh

and the desires of the eyes and pride in possessions—
is not from the Father but is from the world. And
the world is passing away along with its desires, but
whoever does the will of God abides forever. (1 John
2:15–17)

Opportunity

The steps of a man are established by the
LORD,
when he delights in his way;
though he fall, he shall not be cast headlong,
for the LORD upholds his hand. (Ps.
37:23–24)

Whoever works his land will have plenty of
bread,
but he who follows worthless pursuits
lacks sense. (Prov. 12:11)

Commit your work to the LORD,
and your plans will be established. (Prov.
16:3)

> The horse is made ready for the day of battle,
>   but the victory belongs to the LORD. (Prov.
>   21:31)

> Who has spoken and it came to pass,
>   unless the Lord has commanded it?
> Is it not from the mouth of the Most High
>   that good and bad come? (Lam. 3:37–38)

For it will be like a man going on a journey, who called his servants and entrusted to them his property. To one he gave five talents, to another two, to another one, to each according to his ability. Then he went away. He who had received the five talents went at once and traded with them, and he made five talents more. So also he who had the two talents made two talents more. But he who had received the one talent went and dug in the ground and hid his master's money.

Now after a long time the master of those servants came and settled accounts with them. And he who had received the five talents came forward, bringing five talents more, saying, "Master, you delivered to me five talents; here I have made five talents more."

His master said to him, "Well done, good and faithful servant. You have been faithful over a little;

I will set you over much. Enter into the joy of your master."

And he also who had the two talents came forward, saying, "Master, you delivered to me two talents; here I have made two talents more."

His master said to him, "Well done, good and faithful servant. You have been faithful over a little; I will set you over much. Enter into the joy of your master."

He also who had received the one talent came forward, saying, "Master, I knew you to be a hard man, reaping where you did not sow, and gathering where you scattered no seed, so I was afraid, and I went and hid your talent in the ground. Here you have what is yours."

But his master answered him, "You wicked and slothful servant! You knew that I reap where I have not sown and gather where I scattered no seed? Then you ought to have invested my money with the bankers, and at my coming I should have received what was my own with interest. So take the talent from him and give it to him who has the ten talents. For to everyone who has will more be given, and he will have an abundance. But from the one who has not, even what he has will be taken away. And cast the worthless servant into the outer darkness. In that place there will be weeping and gnashing of teeth." (Matt. 25:14–30)

A person cannot receive even one thing unless it is given him from heaven. (John 3:27)

For it is God who works in you, both to will and to work for his good pleasure. (Phil. 2:13)

Michael DiMarco is the bestselling author of *God Guy*, *Devotions for the God Guy*, the *God Guy Bible*, and a number of other books including the 2010 ECPA Christian Book Award winner for youth, *B4UD8* (Before You Date). He is also the publisher and creative director at Hungry Planet, a company his wife Hayley founded and they both operate just outside of Nashville, Tennessee.

You can find Michael at:
Godguy.com
Twitter.com/dimarco
Facebook.com/michael.dimarco

For more of Michael and Hayley's books, visit:
HungryPlanetBooks.com

Hungry Planet helps teens become the people God meant them to be.

Once you become a God Girl or God Guy, your life will never be the same.